Don't Quit

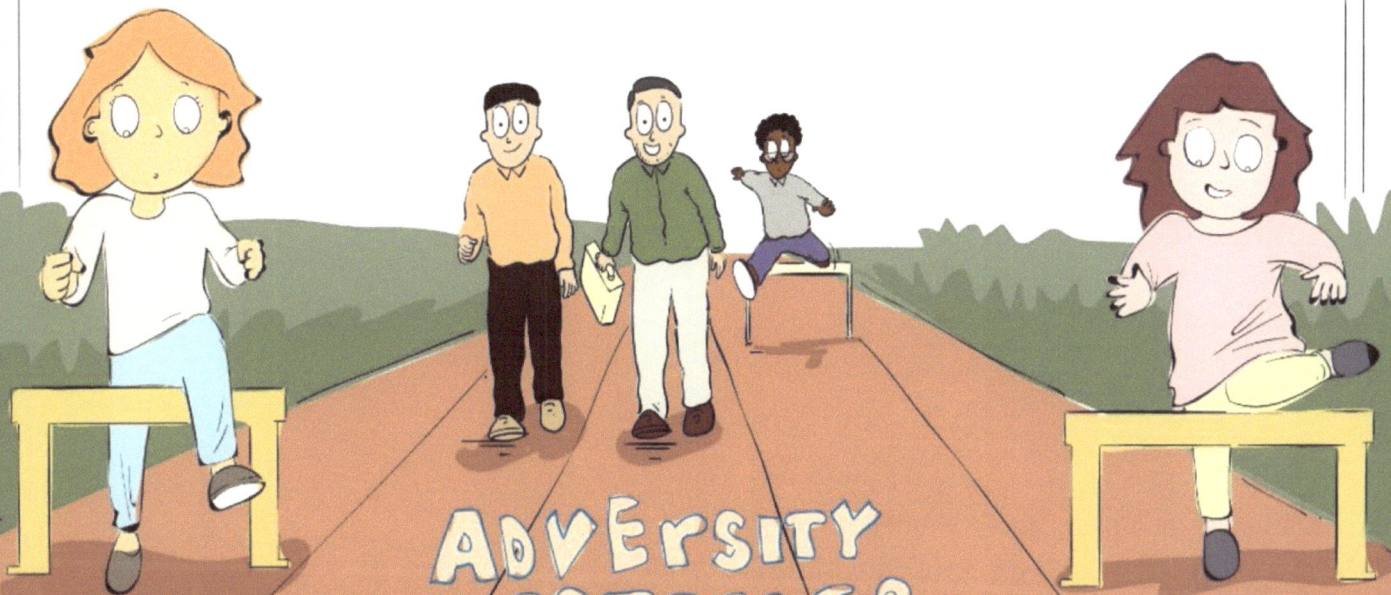

Adversity Obstacles Trials

Michelle McCallum

Published by TJS Publishing House

www.tjspublishinghouse.com
contact@tjspublishinghouse.com

Published in the United States of America
ISBN-13: 978-1-952833-42-7
ISBN-10: 1-952833-42-6

ACKNOWLEDGMENTS

There are so many people that need to be acknowledged for this major accomplishment in my life. First and foremost, I must give God full credit for the publication of book #2. Anything good that comes from me was placed there by God. I am forever thankful for His presence and for Him being a source of constant grace and mercy.

Although you're not here to physically witness the publication and release of this book Ma, I can feel you with me every step of the way. You are certainly the motivation behind the words. Making you proud brings me so much joy. Your children and grandchildren are doing all that we can to keep the memories of you alive.

Angelo Davis, my Daddy, I say to you, although I am not there yet, I am certainly on the way. Thanks for continuing to push me to be all that you and I both know I can be.

I owe infinite thanks to the teachers who believed in me when I didn't believe in myself. Some are no longer with us in the physical, but their love will forever remain with me. I do this because you told me I could. Thanks to all my educators from Allen Jay Elementary, Northeast Middle (now Welborn), T. Wingate Andrews, High Point Central, and the illustrious North Carolina Agricultural and Technical State University for reminding me of the greatness that was in me all along. I will forever be grateful for the role you played in my life.

Ms. Madison Michelle, my teenager, you came along and changed my entire world. You've shown me what it means to love and be loved unconditionally. I fall short each and every day, but please know that each step I make in the right direction is for you! I look at you and see greatness and unlimited possibilities. Thank you for coming along and making me a better person!

Family and friends help make us who we are. No matter how outlandish my dreams and ideas were over the years, my family and friends ALWAYS believed in me and encouraged me to reach for the stars and beyond. I must thank all my family for helping "Chelle" evolve into the person that I am becoming. You consistently told me that there was no limit to what I could do.

Those words didn't fall on deaf ears! I hope that I have and will continue to make you proud.

I must acknowledge my siblings. Shawn, since Mama left us, you and your family have been there for me in ways I could never count. I love and appreciate you and all you do and the man you have become. You're a wonderful father to my nieces, uncle to Madison, and husband to Saundra. I know Mama is proud of you. This is our time! Let's go and get all that is ours, bro!

Shauntai, Tony, and Lo, we have all taken our different routes, but the greatness in each of us is evident. Let's continue to use our God-given talents to leave the world better than we found it. We're Angelo's kids, so we definitely have what it takes to do what the world might see as impossible. Thanks to each of you for selflessly sharing your mom with me over the years. Lil, thanks for loving me like one of your own over the years.

Terry—you continuously apply pressure and push me to be all that I can be. I hate the advice at times, but I know it comes from a good place. Thanks for the continued support you have offered over the years and for the best gift life has ever given me...Madison Michelle Bartley.

To all my educator friends and colleagues, thank you so much for your motivation and for believing in me. Sometimes you describe me with such wonderful words that it sounds like you're talking about a complete stranger. Thanks for seeing in me the person that I don't even see at times. You know who you are. I love and appreciate you all for all you have done for the children and me in your classrooms.

Tonya Joyner (of TJS Publishing House), my awesome publisher, this acknowledgment could never express my gratitude for your professionalism and dedication to the publication process. You made me a published author!!!!!

Finally, to the folks who helped shape me, my family!!! Though we don't always agree, we're still family and there for each other when it counts the most. I wouldn't trade you all for the world! Thanks to all my aunts, uncles, nieces, nephews, and cousins for all that you have done to make me who I am and how you even continue now to help me become a better person. I love you all!!!

Personal Acknowledgments:

I would like to personally acknowledge...

Allen Jay Elementary Teachers and Staff 1984-1989

Northeast Middle School Teachers and Staff 1990-1993

T. Wingate Andrews High School and High Point Central Teachers and Staff, 1993-1997

NC A&T State University Staff, Family, and Friends 1997-2001

My students that I have taught who often believed in me more than I believed in myself.

My awesome coworkers from Kirkman Park, Welborn Middle, Jones Elementary, Southern Middle, and Brightwood Elementary School.

I acknowledge my sister and brothers as well as my nieces, nephews, and cousins.

My friends that have become a part of my extended family.

Angelo Davis and Family

Shauntai Leach and Family

L Rawlings and Family

Jacqueline Buie and Family

Tina B and Family

Johnsie Foster and Family

N. Brewington-McCormick and Family

Phyllis Marshall and Family

Quieta Allen and Family

Marlene Bennett and Family

Dana Harris and Family

Facebook friends and Family

Those who loved my mother and those who she loved

My awesome publisher Tonya Joyner

James McCallum and Family Tony Little and Family

Kristie Wright and Family

My uncles, aunts, and their spouses

Rhonda B and Family

Shesteishia Twyman and Family

Mrs. Curry and Family

Mrs. Dove and Family

T. Stanford and Family

Staci Murray and Family

Carla Clark and Family

Those that randomly check on me

DEDICATION

First and foremost, Ma, this one is for you. The pain of walking this Earth without you has helped me to find a strength I didn't even know I had.

Madison, I often fail at always expressing just how much you mean to me. As I dedicate this book to you, I pray that my actions will show what my words don't always communicate—that I love you more than life itself.

To all my past and future students and teachers, I dedicate this book to you. Jones and Kirkman Park Elementary, Brightwood Elementary, Welborn Middle, Southern Guilford Middle, and Oak View Elementary students, I thank you for allowing me to be a part of your life. I pray that these words and all other words of encouragement I have spoken over your lives will forever resonate with you. Parents who have entrusted me to tutor or teach your child. I can't explain how much it means to me.

If we ever shared a smile, laugh, joke, words of encouragement, or even tears, this book is dedicated to you. Thanks for being a part of my life. I take no one's presence for granted.

Finally, I would like to encourage others through the words of the young. Here are words of wisdom from my daughter and a former student about quitting. They are wise beyond their years.

Madison Bartley—"Quitting is NEVER a good thing to do, especially before you actually try something. If you give up on something without trying it, you could miss out on several opportunities in life."

Na'Vaeh Stanford "Trying is the key to success. You can inspire so many people through the little things that you do, even if your actions feel meaningless at the time. Always try! In the end, it's all worth it. Keep going, and don't quit!

Don't Quit

Michelle McCallum

Life gets rough sometimes, and folks won't always treat you fair,

But you must stay in the race, never quit, don't you dare!

Take a break if you must, and come up with another plan,

But quitting isn't an option, fulfill your purpose like only you can.

Times will get tough, and you will want to put your head down in despair,

But you must remain in the race of life, never quit, don't you dare!

Tears will fall, and it will seem like you can't go on anymore,

But when you least expect it, you'll find a strength you didn't possess before.

Life will present several challenges, causing you to throw your hands in the air,

But you must remain steadfast in the race of life, never quit, don't you dare!

Trials will come, and it will be hard to hold on at times,

Just when it seems hopeless, life will reveal its perfect design.

You'll look back and remember when you were almost convinced you didn't care,

And be reminded that you must endure this race of life. Never quit. Don't you dare!

Perils will surely come, and at times, you'll think you're all alone, and no one understands your battle,

Only to find that the strength you've gained from your trials gave you the will to stay in the saddle.

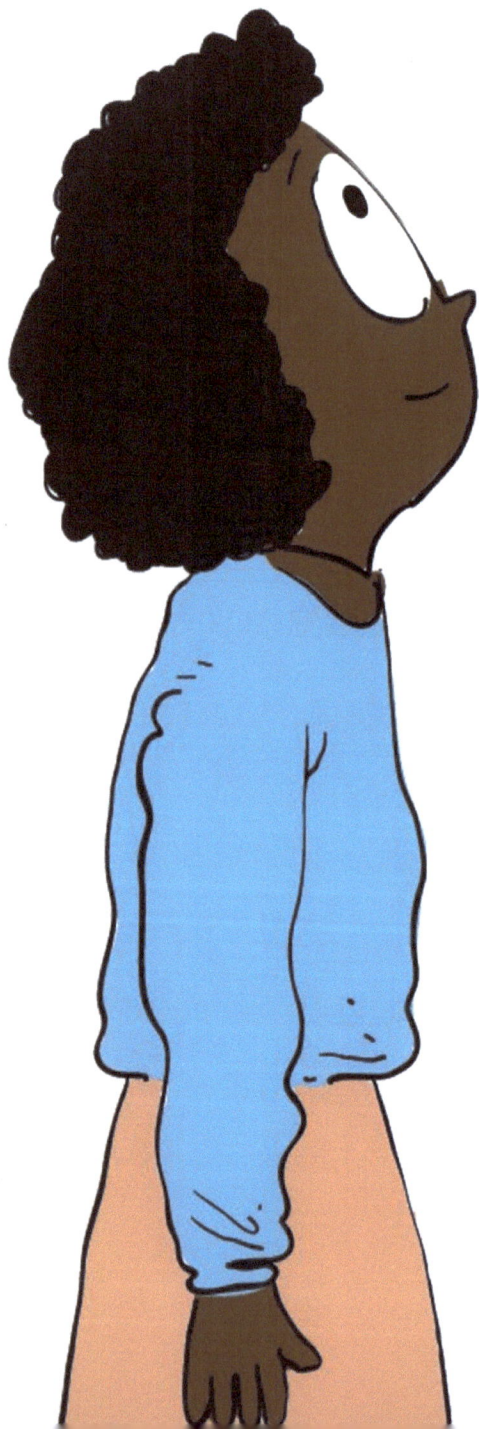

So, I say to you once more, it won't always be easy, but God is always there,

You mustn't quit this race called life. Don't you dare!

ABOUT THE AUTHOR

Michelle McCallum was born and raised in High Point, NC. She's a graduate of the wonderful North Carolina A&T State University. She has worked as an educator for over 15 years, teaching elementary and middle school. She has an avid love for reading and teaching reading. Her words are inspired by God, and she hopes to encourage anyone who ever finds themselves where she once found herself—lost without a clue of what life held for her.

She is a mother to a beautiful daughter, Madison Michelle Bartley, and the proud aunt of many nieces and nephews.

www.ingramcontent.com/pod-product-compliance
Lightning Source LLC
LaVergne TN
LVHW072132070426
835513LV00002B/76